Gordon
gordonj.reason@virgin.net

Moods of the

BRONTË MOORS

THE MILLS AND MOORS OF THE SOUTH PENNINES

JOHN MORRISON

HALSGROVE

First published in Great Britain in 2004

Title page photograph: The Rochdale Canal is helping to bring new life to South Pennine milltowns such as Hebden Bridge.

British Library Cataloguing-in-Publication Data
A CIP record for this title is available from the British Library

ISBN 1 84114 351 0

HALSGROVE
Halsgrove House
Lower Moor Way
Tiverton, Devon EX16 6SS
Tel: 01884 243242
Fax: 01884 243325
email: sales@halsgrove.com
website: www.halsgrove.com

Printed and bound by D'Auria Industrie Grafiche Spa, Italy

INTRODUCTION

The South Pennines lie between the Yorkshire Dales to the north and the Peak District to the south. But, unlike these national parks, the South Pennines have no distinct boundary. They don't even respect the county borders, which creates an obvious affinity between the milltowns of West Yorkshire and East Lancashire, and the moors which surround them.

The uplands are riven by steep-sided, wooded valleys – known locally as 'cloughs' – of which the best-known example is Hardcastle Crags. 'Hebden Bridge for the Crags,' was the station master's cry as steam trains pulled into Hebden Bridge each weekend. The millhands of the industrial towns were heading to Hardcastle Crags for picnics and riverside strolls at a time when Hebden Bridge itself was just another smoky little milltown.

Plenty of places like to call themselves 'The Cradle of Industry', but the South Pennines are one of the few to have a genuine claim. When the spinning and weaving of wool and cotton were transferred from cottage loomshops to the mills, this is where it happened – rapidly and traumatically. A century ago, there were 33 mills in Hebden Bridge, a town the size of a village. So hilly was the terrain that the millhands lived in houses that were built, quite literally, on top of each other.

The history of the South Pennines is written in the crowded valleys and on the brow of every hill. Road, railway, river and canal cross and recross each other along the Calderdale valley, like the braided flex of an old-fashioned telephone. Haworth, a few miles to the north, is where the Brontë sisters honed the precocious writing skills that would flower in novels such as *Wuthering Heights* and *The Tenant of Wildfell Hall*.

One great attraction of the area is the proximity of town and country. You can shut the door of your 'top and bottom' house, walk up a cobbled ginnel and, five minutes later, be striding out across the breezy moortops with only curlews and cotton grass for company. Every few minutes walking will bring a new and surprising panorama to enjoy.

This is no pastoral idyll. I've heard the area described as being 'dark and fierce', which may give a clue to why the people who like the South Pennines tend to like them a lot, and why the people who don't tend to shake their heads uncomprehendingly. I'm a big fan of this idiosyncratic landscape; count me in.

John Morrison

LOCATION MAP

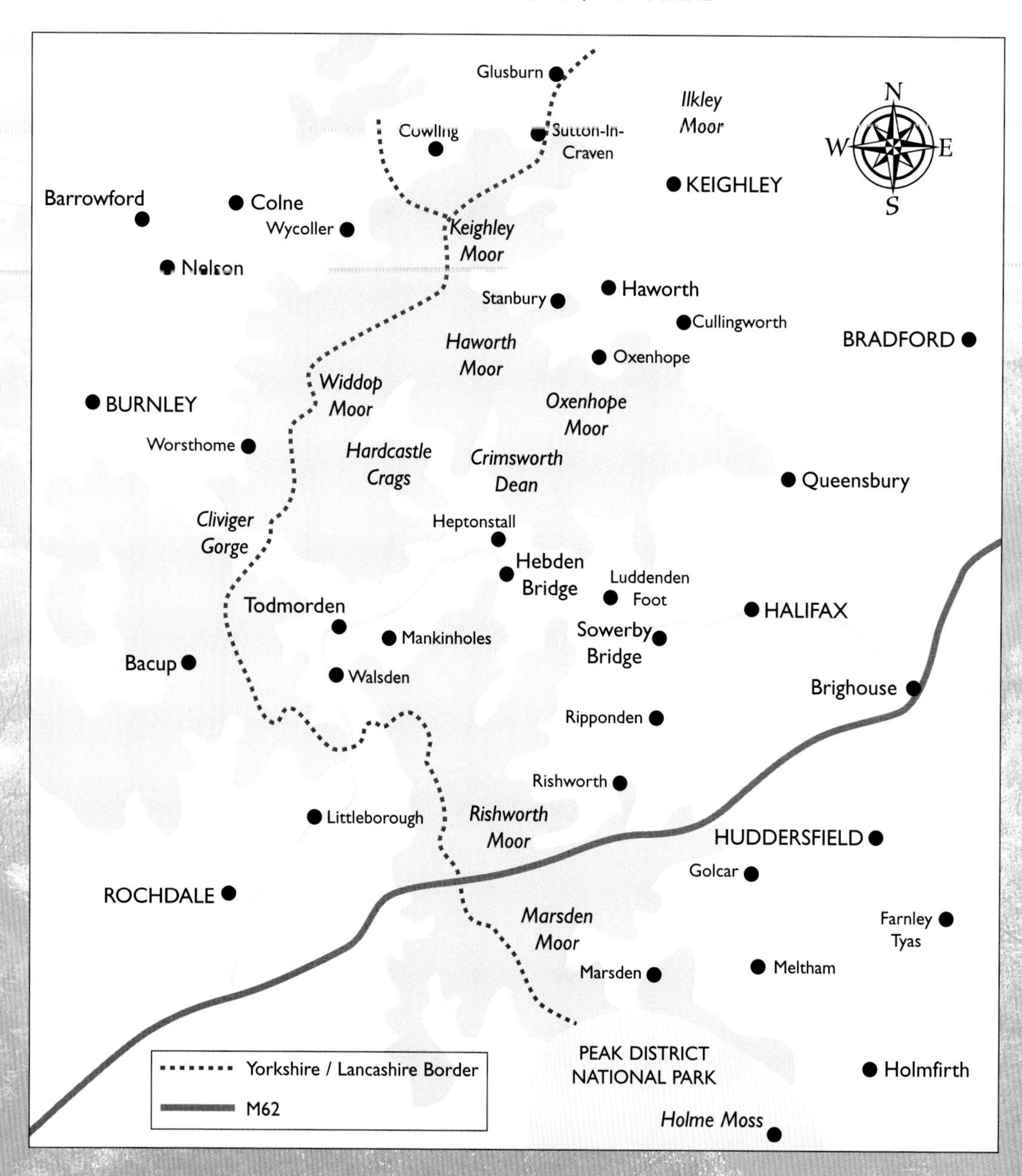

Water from the mill dams used to power the earliest textile mills in the South Pennines; now they are oases for wildlife.

Above: The marina of the Rochdale Canal at Sowerby Bridge: once unloved and unwanted, but now being given a major facelift.

Right: High summer in Hebden Bridge, when systems analysts and estate agents can pretend they are bold bargees.

Hardcastle Crags is the venue each summer for a sculpture trail, where familar views are given a creative twist.

A long and winding road that
leads to a farmhouse near Stanbury.

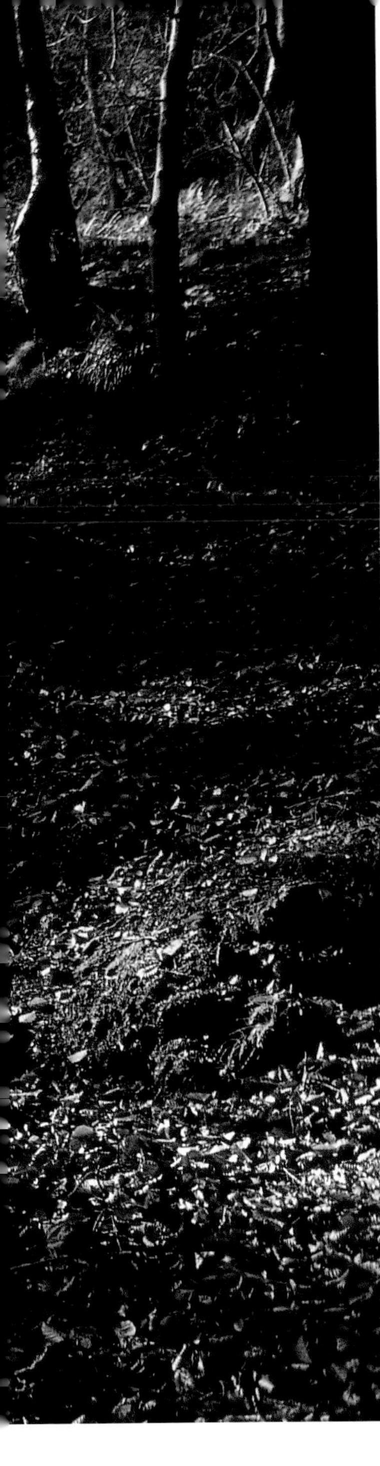

Above: 'The Crags' are beautiful at any time of year,
but autumnal colours are particularly attractive.

Left: Light and shade in the woodland of Hardcastle Crags,
and a leaf-strewn path that begs to be explored.

Above: Buckstones, a breezy escarpment on the Pennine watershed, is a popular venue for hang-gliding and parascending.

Right: After take-off an ungainly, Heath-Robinson arrangement of struts and wires and canvas becomes a graceful aerofoil.

Above: The flowers carpeting the fields of this Calderdale scene indicate that it is early summer, before the first mowing.

Left: Sunlight sparkles on the River Calder, one of the hardest-worked rivers in Yorkshire, but here looking unusually placid.

Above: The side-valleys of Calderdale, known as 'cloughs', are well-wooded – not with gloomy conifer plantations, but with oak, ash and beech.

Left: Hardcastle Crags, a traditional escape route into the countryside, when cramped milltowns become claustrophobic.

Hollingworth Lake, near Littleborough, was known as 'The Weavers' Seaport':
a sort of inland resort for the millhands of the industrial towns.

The Rochdale Canal on its approach into Todmorden – with the ubiquitous monument of Stoodley Pike in the distance.

THE WHITE SWAN

Above: The candyfloss colours of springtime blossom help to soften the gritstone scene in Hebden Bridge.

Left: The sixteenth century, three-arched packhorse bridge over the River Hebden which gave the town of Hebden Bridge its name.

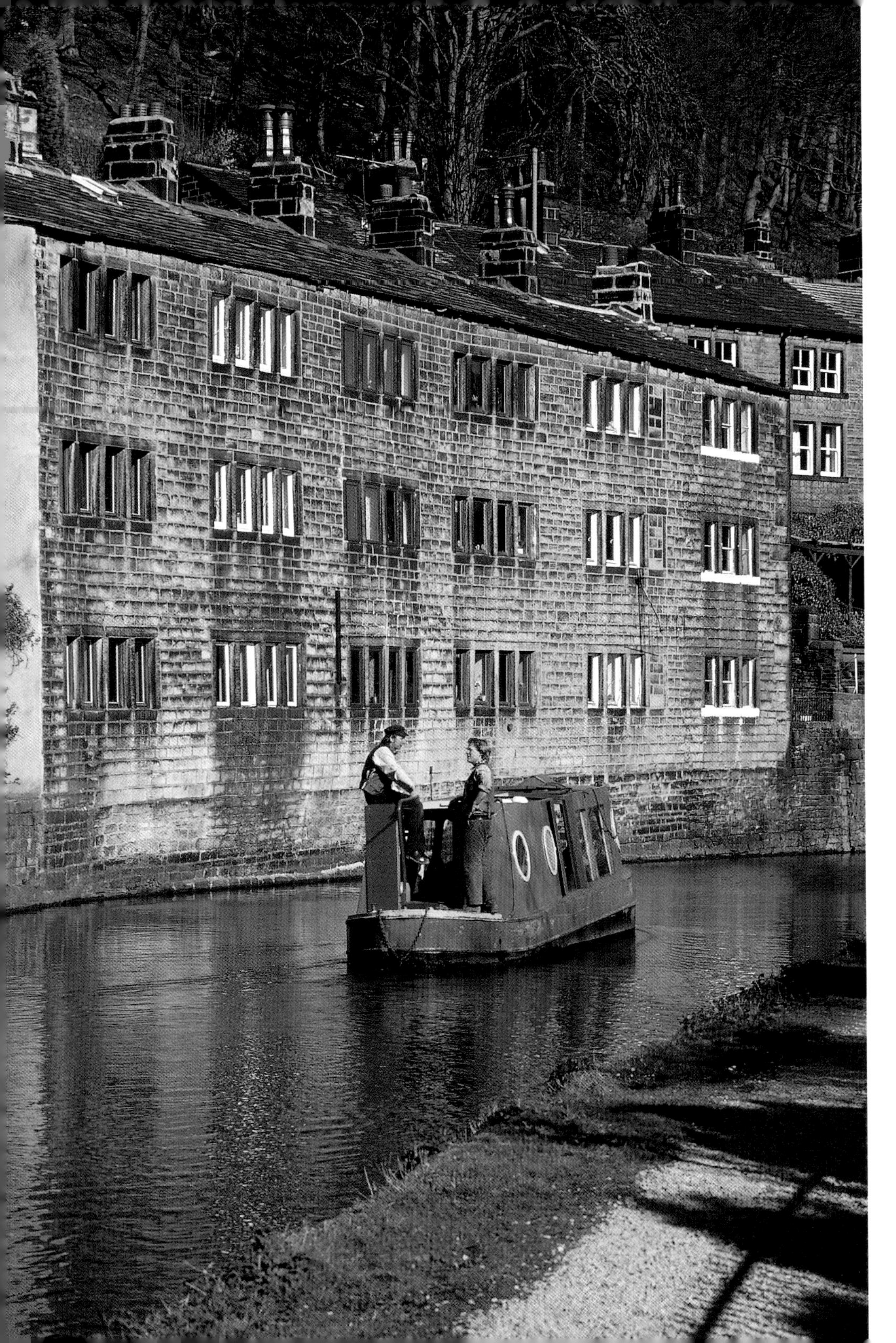

The twenty first century barely intrudes on this timeless scene on the Rochdale Canal.

In a bizarre example of municipal vandalism, the Rochdale Canal was filled in at Sowerby Bridge: a situation now happily rectified.

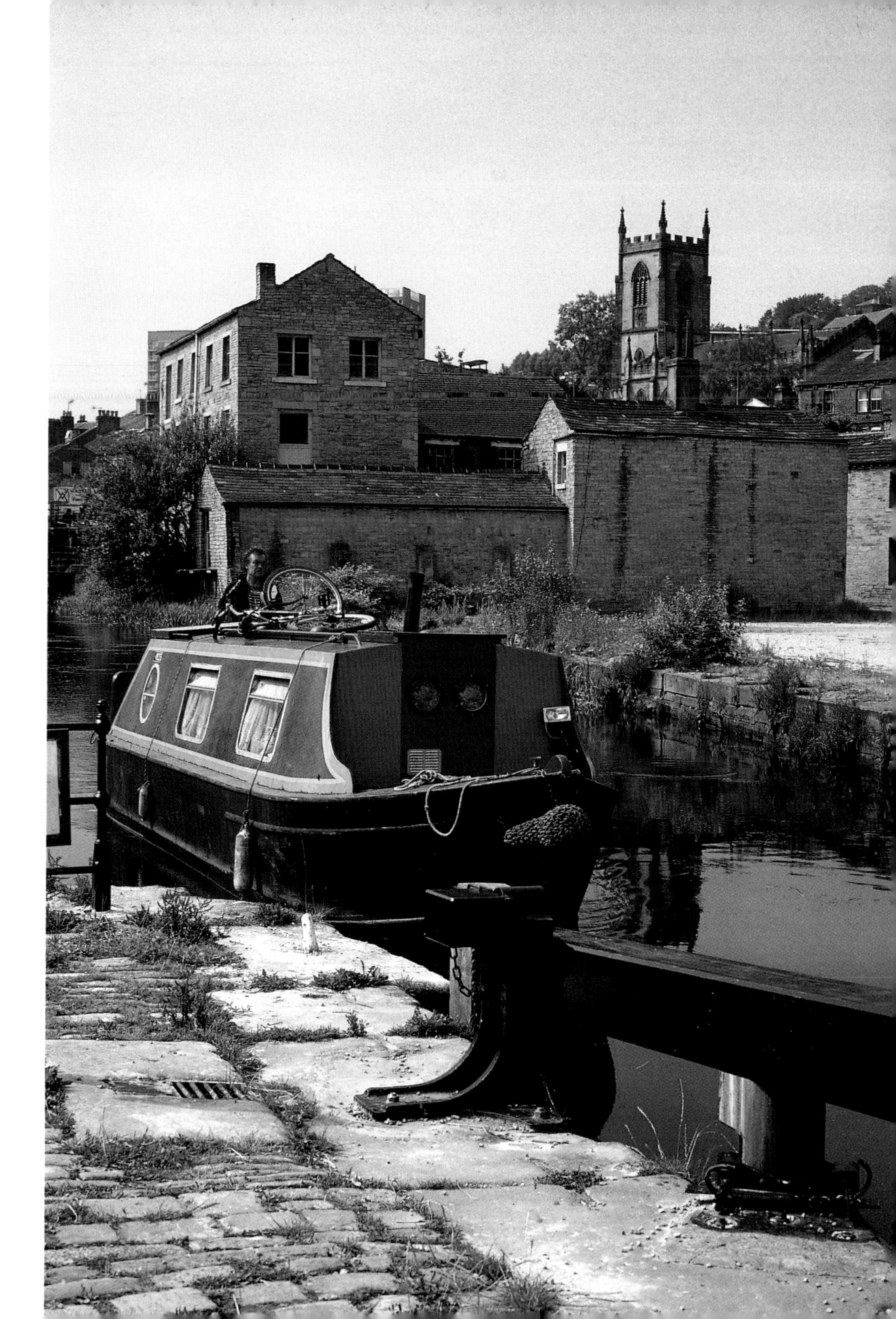

Above: Oakwell Hall, a splendid example of a sixteenth century manor house, was immortalised by Charlotte Brontë as 'Fieldhead' in her novel, *Shirley*.

Left: Park Hill, a well-preserved, seventeenth century house in Barrowford, which is now the Pendle Heritage Centre.

The windfarms that have sprung up on breezy Pennine outcrops have divided opinions...

...Even the Green lobby can't agree whether they are intrusive
eyesores or represent an 'environmentally friendly' future.

Erected on Langfield Edge in 1814, Stoodley Pike commemorated the end of the Napoleonic War.

Stoodley Pike is the most visible of the many memorials and obelisks erected on exposed sites in Calderdale.

Above: Evening light picks out an old waymarking stone in Peckett Well.

Left: Mild architectural eccentricity is not uncommon in the South Pennines.

Above: The sun slips below the silhouette of Castle Hill, as prominent a landmark in Kirklees as Stoodley Pike is in Calderdale.

Left: A hot-air balloon takes off from Castle Hill, offering some lucky people an unforgettable panorama of the Pennine hills.

Above: The slate roofs of Colne, a Lancashire town built on cotton, with the distinctive profile of Pendle Hill as a backdrop.

Left: A shaft of sunlight permeates the gloom, creating rainbows and picking out rows of terraced cottages near Colne.

Above: Shibden Hall, near Halifax, whose most famous owner was Anne Lister: candid diarist and outspoken feminist.

Right: A sturdy farmhouse in the Luddenden Valley, with the date carved proudly on the door lintel.

1624

Above: Cruising in high summer along the Rochdale Canal, on the approach to Todmorden.

Right: A narrowboat proceeding at a convivial pace along the Calder and Hebble Navigation, at Selterhebble, near Halifax.

Above: A quartet of climbers preparing to tackle one of the rock faces at the Cow and Calf Rocks.

Left: The famous Cow and Calf Rocks overlooking Ilkley
(there used to be a Bull as well, but it was broken up for building stone).

Beyond the cramped confines of the Calder Valley lie mile after mile of open moorland; this is the old road to Haworth.

Striding across the expanse of Haworth Moor, with the ruins of Top Withins in the background.

Above: A grassy path leading away from Hardcastle Crags, towards the well-known picnic site of Blake Dean.

Right: The familiar silhouette of Pendle Hill, viewed from the top of Boulsworth Hill.

Above: A strong wind blows snow from the top of Holme Moss:
where the South Pennines end and the Peak District National Park begins.

Left: A compact cluster of fine old houses – known as Saltonstall – in the Luddenden Valley

Above: The South Pennines are criss-crossed with a network of good paths and tracks, making for great walking country.

Left: Some old tracks have been upgraded for motor traffic;
others, like this one near Holmfirth, are still available to walkers.

Above: A typical South Pennine scene in Calderdale: neat fields, copses and scattered farms.

Right: It's good to lace up the walking boots and head for open country...
especially when the traffic on the M62 is gridlocked at Scammonden Bridge.

A shaft of sunlight picks out a neat row of walled fields, near Hepworth, with Castle Hill on the horizon.

Fields won from the surrounding moorland sweep down from the heights of Langfield Common, near Todmorden.

Above: Spring comes to a long laith-house, overlooking the Crimsworth Valley: a traditional dwelling with living quarters and barn under one roof.

Left: A farmhouse of uncompromising design near Colden, built to withstand the worst of Pennine weather.

Above: Freshly-mown fields create intriguing patterns behind an old house near Slaithwaite in Kirklees.

Right: Near Cowling; a typical North Country scene, with drystone walls dividing up the landscape into fields of irregular shape and size.

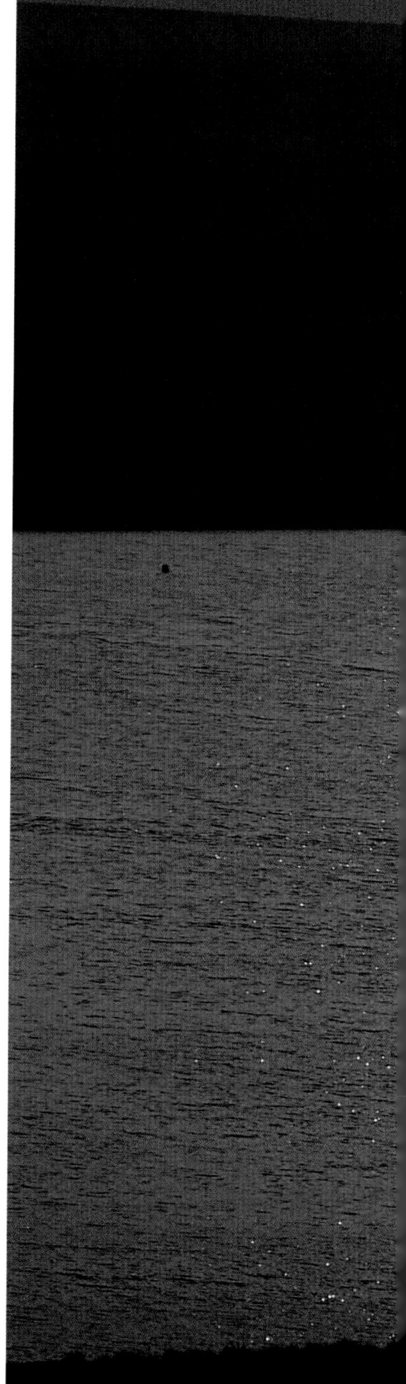

Above: Youngsters having fun in pint-sized dinghies on Boshaw Whams Reservoir, near Holmfirth.

Right: Sailing boats gliding across the water of Warley Moor Reservoir, made molten by evening light.

Haworth can be unbearably crowded in summer; avoid the throng, and feel the atmosphere, by coming in winter.

Sunlight, filtered through the mist, creates a sense of theatre in the old graveyard of Haworth church.

Great Rock, between Todmorden and Hebden Bridge, is a landmark familiar to walkers along the 50-mile Calderdale Way.

The Bridestones: gritstone outcrops, 'on the tops' above Todmorden, with this gravity-defying rock as the centrepiece.

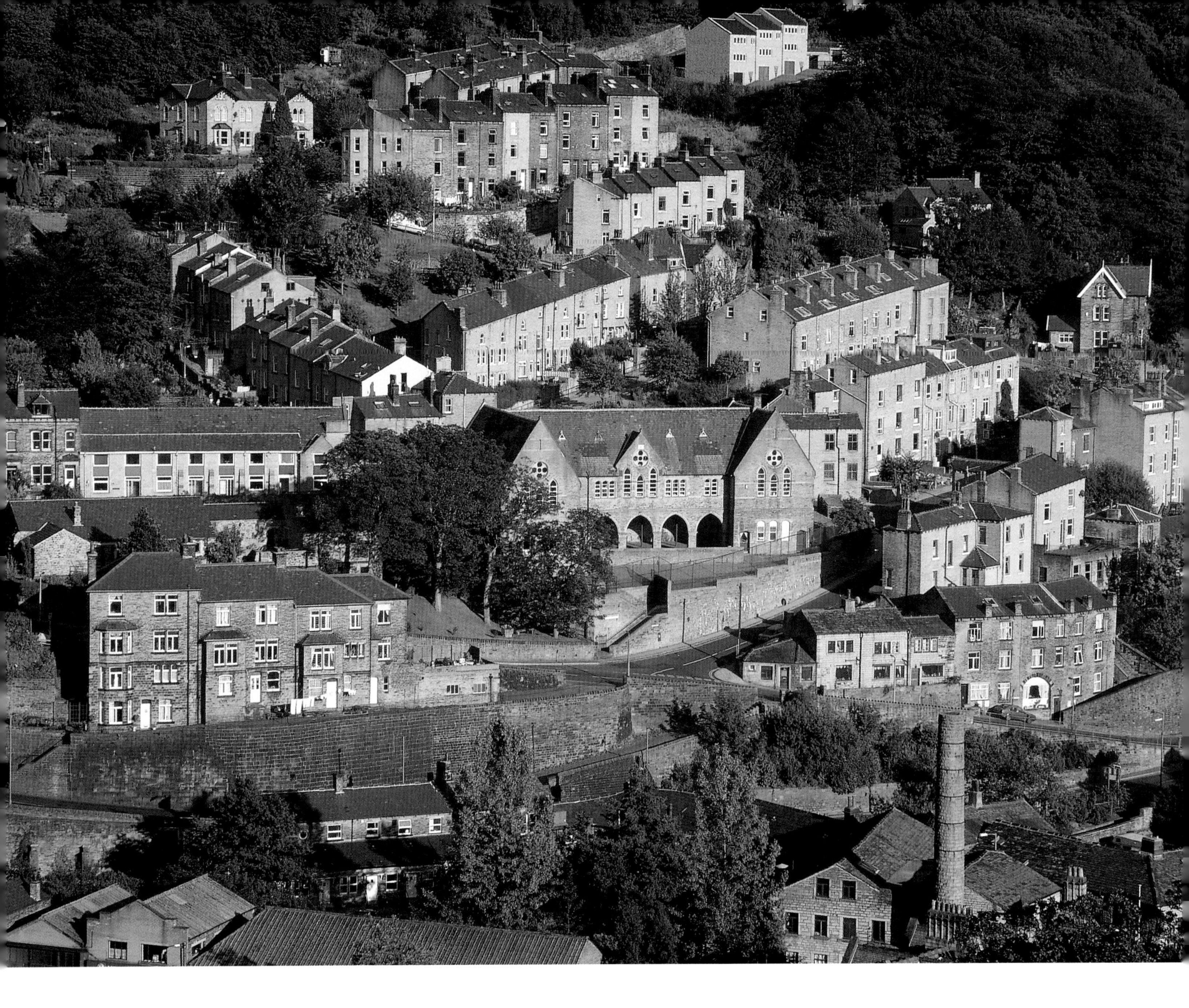

Above: The Stubbings area of Hebden Bridge – with Stubbings School at the centre – creates an intriguing pattern when viewed from the Heptonstall Road.

Left: 'Top and bottom' houses in Hebden Bridge, with one house built on top of another: an imaginitive response to the hilly terrain.

Above: Heptonstall Church rises head and shoulders above the gritstone houses,
to be silhouetted against snowy Pennine hills.

Left: The first snowfall of winter in Hebden Bridge: like a light sprinkling of icing sugar on the patchwork of roofs.

Above: The lock-keeper's cottage on the Rochdale Canal, near Summit – on the Pennine watershed between Yorkshire and Lancashire.

Right: Motorists who drive through Ripponden, on their way to the motorway, will miss this gem of a pub, the venerable Bridge Inn.

Above: Golcar, now a suburb of Huddersfield, used to known for hand-weaving; the attic rooms with rows of narrow windows were the loomshops.

Left: The road, railway and Rochdale Canal are shoehorned tightly into the valley bottom at Todmorden.

The Pennine hills remained a formidable barrier to travel until the M62 was sliced, at great expense, across inhospitable moorland.

Evening light is reflected in the surface of Booth Wood Reservoir, as the motorway rises up to Saddleworth Moor.

Above: On the moors above Todmorden, a pink-tongued lamb unaccountably mistook me for its mother.

Right: A pair of sheep that posed for the camera – albeit briefly – against the empty expanse of Keighley Moor.

Thanks to the long-running TV comedy *Last of the Summer Wine*, this unremarkable terraced house in Holmfirth is known as the house where Nora Batty lives.

Holmfirth is full of ginnels, snickets and hidden corners like this, where a young couple can relax and enjoy an ice cream.

Above: People flock to Hebden Bridge on sunny summer days – to relax, stroll along the canal and feed the ducks.

Left: A tranquil stretch of canal, a moored-up narrowboat and a bridge of traditional design, on the Rochdale Canal near Mytholmroyd.

Above: Winter comes to the Pennine hills; even with global warming, the trans-Pennine roads are blocked most years.

Left: Stoodley Pike stands out on a clear winter's day in Calderdale.

Above: Spectral figures fade into the gloom, as mist envelops the famous cobbled street in Haworth.

Left: Walkers stride out along the ridge of Langfield Edge, which offers panoramic views across Calderdale.

Above: Early morning at Gibson's Mill, in Hardcastle Crags: belying the sylvan setting, young children worked long hours here for meagre pay.

Right: Not an optical illusion, but a site-specific sculpture – highlighting the mill's reflection with artfully-arranged ropes.

An archetypal South Pennine view: a stone farmhouse, the old hilltop village of Heptonstall and the admonishing finger of Stoodley Pike.

Warm light on a summer's evening, with the distinctive outline of Heptonstall church in the distance.

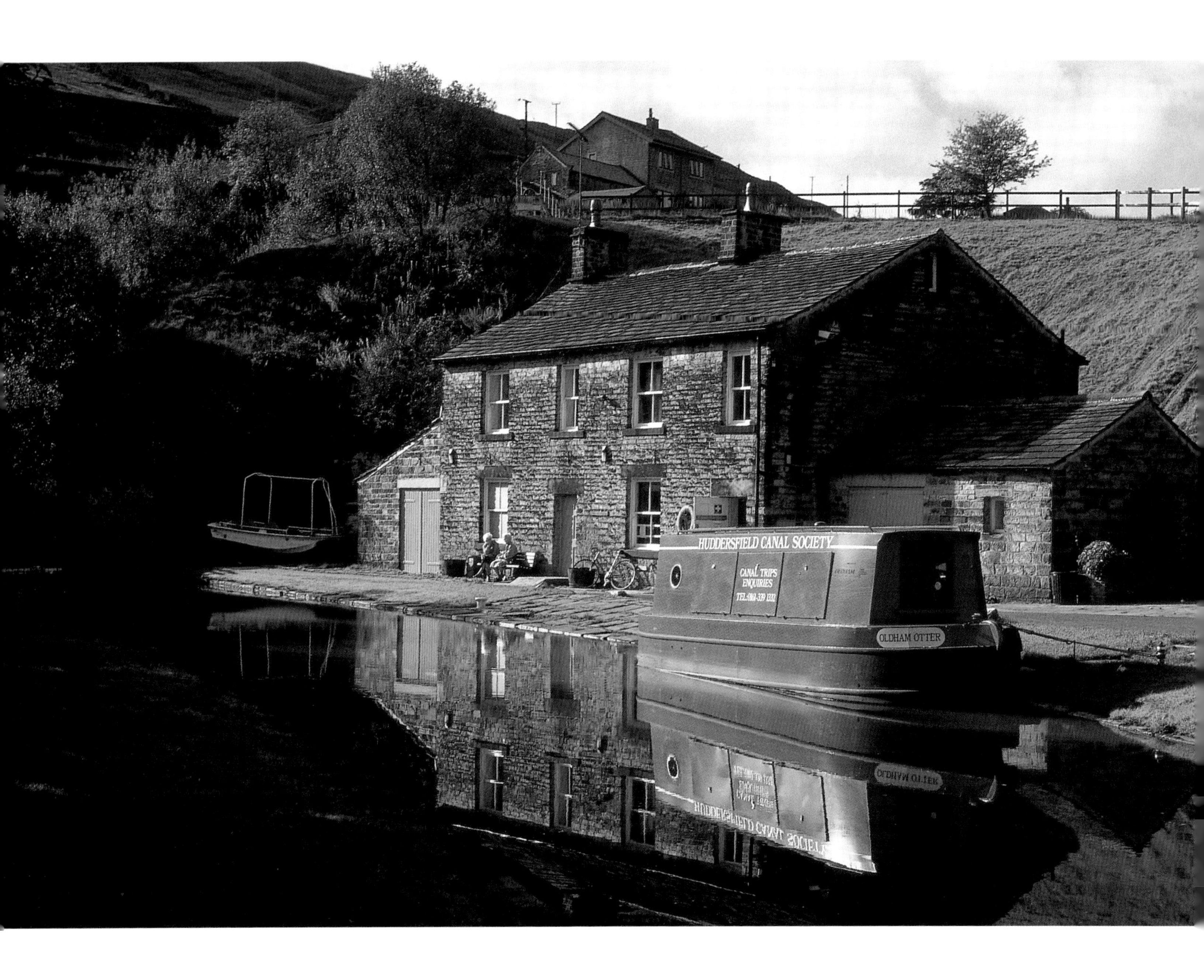

HUDDERSFIELD CANAL SOCIETY
CANAL TRIPS
ENQUIRIES
OLDHAM OTTER

Above: The old tollhouse in Barrowford: an intriguing relic of the turnpike road system.

Left: An older picture of Tunnel End, near Marsden, where the recently-restored Huddersfield Narrow Canal goes underground for 3 gloomy miles, and re-emerges in Lancashire.

Blake Dean and Hebden Water: a site of industry while a trio of reservoirs were being built, now peaceful walking country once again.

The close proximity of town and country: within a few minutes of leaving Marsden and its mills, you can be out 'on the tops'.

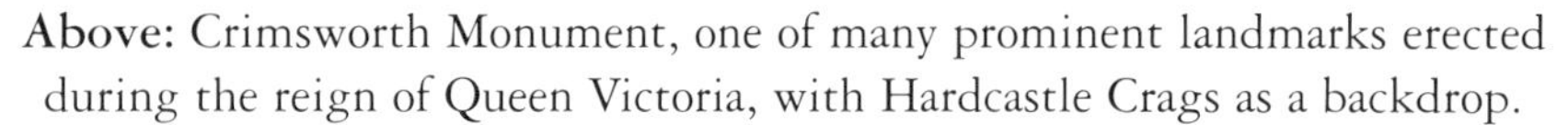

Above: Crimsworth Monument, one of many prominent landmarks erected during the reign of Queen Victoria, with Hardcastle Crags as a backdrop.

Right: The Brontë Parsonage in Haworth, where Charlotte, Emily and Anne perfected their literary skills.

Above: Farming at higher altitudes proved unsustainable; abandoned farmsteads can be found throughout the South Pennines.

Left: A splash of sunlight picks out a farmhouse in rolling country near Cowling; in the distance are the Dales of North Yorkshire.

Above: Though you wouldn't guess from this picture, Hebden Water powered a number of mill waterwheels before meeting the River Calder.

Left: This splendid little waterfall can be found after a pleasant stroll along Harden Beck.

Above: Fields of crushed velvet, near Shepley in Kirklees.

Left: The Brontë sisters would have been familiar with this old farmhouse, near Haworth, but not with Leeshaw Reservoir.

Hebden Bridge is a place where hippy ideals, artistic pursuits and mild eccentricity create a relaxed atmosphere.

One of these days the good people of Halifax will realise what a gem they have in the Piece Hall: a monumental example of pre-industrial architecture.

The Huddersfield Narrow Canal, near Slaithwaite: a haven of tranquility linking the milltowns of the Colne Valley.

There's mile after mile of easy, level walking along the Huddersfield Narrow Canal.

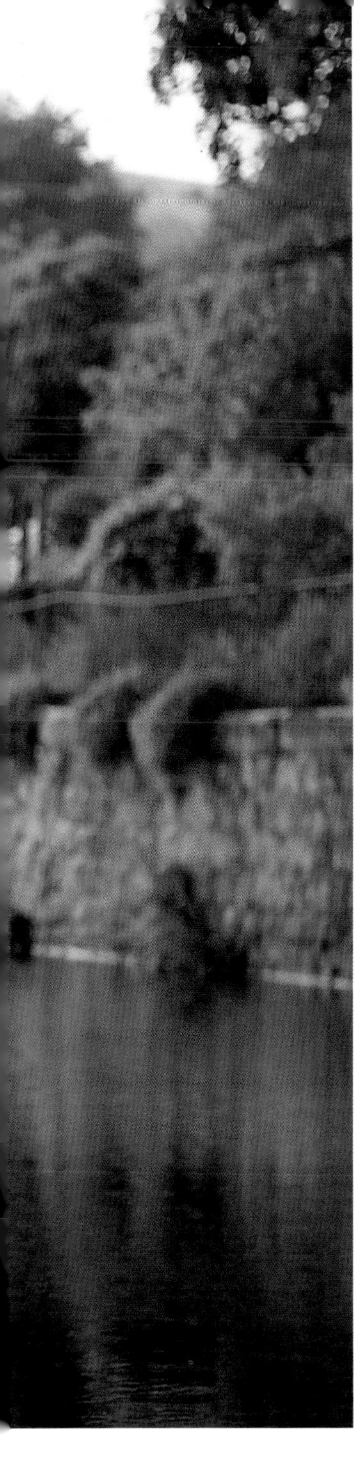

Left: A pair of geese pose obligingly on the bank of the Rochdale Canal, in Hebden Bridge.

Above: Still posing... against the reflections of a narrowboat shattered into colourful abstraction.

Above: Being bearded, slightly overweight and with no sense of rhythm, it's only a matter of time before I take up Morris dancing.

Right: The Sowerby Bridge Rushbearing Festival involves carting a haystack around narrow South Pennine lanes.

BRIDGE

The Colne Royal Morris Men bring colour, music and embarrassing headgear to Weaver's Square, in Heptonstall.

The Pace Egg Play is perfomed in Heptonstall on Good Friday, with characters such as St George, Bold Slasher and – here – an *idiot savant* called Tosspot.

Above: An isolated farmhouse near Blake Dean, where the wooded Hebden Valley opens out into moorland.

Left: Ragged stone walls define the fields of long abandoned farmsteads, on the flank of Crimsworth Dean.

Above: This pastoral scene looks timeless, except for the sliver of motorway – the M62 – at the top right, and Scammonden Reservoir, just out of shot.

Left: Burnley, another Lancashire town built on cotton, framed by the bulk of Pendle Hill.

Above: The compact, pre-industrial hamlet of Mankinholes is little changed from when this cottage was built, three centuries ago.

Left: An ancient landscape, old houses and, beyond the Luddenden Valley, the rather more modern addition of a windfarm.

Thanks to its status as a Conservation Area, the hill village of Heptonstall hasn't been ruined by inappropriate development.

Heptonstall was an important centre for hand-woven cloth at a time when Hebden Bridge, in the valley below, was little more than a river crossing.

Above: It's hard to differentiate between commercial premises and 'top and bottom' houses in the cramped confines of Hebden Bridge.

Right: It's a similar story a few miles down-river, at Sowerby Bridge, where houses and mills are crowded along the River Calder.

JOEL
HOUSE
CORAL

Above: Bridgeholme Cricket Club enjoys an enviable position, with Stoodley Pike appearing in a gap in the Calderdale hills.

Left: Cock Hill is the highest point on the old road from Hebden Bridge to Haworth, and offers bright and breezy walking.

Above: From the vantage of Beacon Hill, Halifax is spread out below: a living history of the Industrial Revolution and beyond.

Right: Muck and brass in Milnsbridge: those more accustomed to the leafy lanes of the Home Counties may find these northern milltowns a bit tatty.

A peaceful morning on the canal towpath in Hebden Bridge, with blossom on the boughs.

The authors of an early tourism brochure suggested that visitors wouldn't come until the canal was filled in; they couldn't have been more wrong.

Above: The view from Langfield Common, towards the town of Todmorden, and into Lancashire.

Left: An old packhorse causeway – stones fitting together as snugly as jigsaw pieces – leading down into Mankinholes and Lumbutts.

Above: The Basin Stone, a distinctive landmark on the tops above Walsden, was used as an open-air pulpit by travelling Methodist ministers.

Left: Walking country at its best – near Todmorden – with a new view opening up every few minutes to reward your efforts.

The last rays of evening light illuminate the lock-keeper's cottage and a mill chimney on the outskirts of Todmorden.

A typical South Pennine scene: a sturdy gritsone house, a walled path, a scattering of farms and – seldom far away – a mill chimney.

Above: A walled track of a kind found throughout the South Pennines; this one leads down into Mytholmroyd.

Left: A view across fields to Keighley (pronounce it 'Keith-ley', not 'Kee-ley', if you want to sound like a local).

David Hartley was the leader of the Cragg Vale Coiners, hanged for clipping the edges of gold coins. This is his gravestone in Heptonstall churchyard.

Redolent of the days when traffic travelled at a horse's pace, this old fingerpost stands at a fork in the road near Heptonstall.

Above: The last milltown in the Colne Valley; beyond Marsden is the bleak Pennine watershed of Standedge.

Left: A Huddersfield millscape, with Emley Moor TV mast dominating the horizon.

There are plenty of narrow, cobbled streets in villages such as Luddenden, planned and built for people and horses rather than cars.

Typical terraced houses in Harden of a type found throughout the South Pennines:
sturdy, unpretentious and with a certain rugged charm.

Above: Manning the locks for a pair of approaching narrowboats on the Rochdale Canal in Hebden Bridge.

Left: A dinghy adds a splash of colour to this canal-side scene near Littleborough.

Above: A pair of wayside crosses of unusual design, known as Abel Cross, guarding the entrance to the Crimsworth Valley.

Right: An old mill dam in Luddendean Dean becomes a little haven for wildlife, now that the mill it used to serve has been silenced.

Evening light creates warm reflections in the Rochdale Canal.